# Grammar Puzzles & Games Kids Can't Resist!

## 40 Super-Cool Crosswords, Codes, Mazes & More
## That Teach the Essential Rules of Grammar

by Karen Kellaher

SCHOLASTIC
PROFESSIONAL BOOKS

New York ★ Toronto ★ London ★ Auckland ★ Sydney
Mexico City ★ New Delhi ★ Hong Kong

# Dedication

**To Colin
for all your love and support**

**And special thanks to Mr. Ed Miller,
who made grammar fun for me**

Edited by Sylvia Charlesworth
Cover design by Jaime Lucero
Cover illustration by Mike Moran
Interior design by Grafica, Inc.
Interior illustration by Mike Moran

ISBN: 0-439-07756-7

# Contents

# Contents

# Introduction

There is something about games and puzzles that motivates even the most reluctant learner. We see this clearly when we look at our own habits: As adults, few of us would jump at the chance to take a test on world history, literature, science, or geography. However, we rush to answer questions in these subject areas when they're part of a trivia board game, TV quiz show, or Sunday newspaper crossword puzzle. Why? I believe it's because the idea of a game or puzzle lends an exciting context to learning, and we achieve a real sense of accomplishment when we get the answers right.

Children are no exception. When subject matter is part of a game or puzzle, students are more motivated to learn, to remember, and to apply the material. That's the thinking behind *Grammar Puzzles & Games Kids Can't Resist!*

## Why Use Grammar Games?

At Scholastic we recognize that grammar is not the easiest topic to teach. Too often, grammar seems like a collection of rules that must be memorized. Students have a hard time seeing its relevance to real life. And teachers sometimes have a difficult time changing students from the comfortable—but incorrect—grammar habits which the kids are used to using. It is our hope that *Grammar Puzzles & Games Kids Can't Resist!* will make the teaching of grammar a little bit easier and a lot more fun. You'll find crossword puzzles, word searches, code games, partner stories, and more. These are entertaining activities that children already love to do, so consider your battle half won!

Some of the special features of this book include:

★ **Grammar "fast facts" with every activity.** These reminders review the specific grammar concept the children need for each activity—right there on the reproducible. For example, when students are working with helping verbs, they'll find a list of helping verbs right there on the page. When they are working with proper nouns, they'll find a helpful reminder to always use a capital letter. That means your students will not have to look elsewhere for pertinent information.

★ **Opportunities for both independent and collaborative learning.** Some of the activities—such as crosswords and word searches—are designed for students to complete individually. Others—such as the partner stories—are meant to be tackled in pairs or teams.

★ **Special attention to typical problem areas.** As veteran teachers know, some grammar rules are more troublesome than others. For example, many children have a hard time forming contractions, forming the past tense of irregular verbs, and choosing the homonym that makes sense in a sentence. This book addresses these tough topics clearly and decisively.

## How to Use the Book

You may use the reproducible activities in any order. Here are some suggestions for making the most of them:

1. Use each reproducible as an immediate follow-up to a grammar lesson to assess what students have learned. Because the activities include very simple instructions and grammar rule reminders, you can easily assign the activities as homework. I can assure you that your students won't mind digging into these assignments!

2. Use the reproducibles as part of a Grammar Learning Center where the focus changes each week. For example, while you are teaching about nouns, you may want to copy all of the activities that focus on nouns and store the activities in a designated spot in the classroom. Send students to the Grammar Learning Center when they finish work early, when you are working with small groups, or any other time individual students are looking for something to do. Invite students to make colorful posters of important grammar rules and use them to decorate your Learning Center.

3. Consider having students check their own work. (Use the answer key on page 58 to post the answers on the board.) Then work with each student to highlight and focus on any problem areas.

4. After students have completed the puzzles for a given grammar topic, invite them to create their own puzzles for classmates to work on. Younger students will enjoy making word search puzzles and simple crosswords on graph paper. Older students may want to try crafting their own riddle bubble tests and partner stories. (In either case, take a peek at the student-made activities before students exchange them. This will help avoid frustration in the event that a student-created puzzle is incorrect or incomplete.)

# About the Puzzle Formats: A Special Note to Teachers

Each of the puzzles in this book includes easy-to-follow directions. The puzzles are broken down as follows:

## Word Searches
Students hunt for their answers in a letter grid. Answers may go across, down, or on the diagonal.

## Snails
In these puzzles, the answers wrap around in the shape of a snail. The last letter of one answer is the first letter of the next.

## Crosswords
These crosswords are designed simply with elementary students in mind. All of the clues and answers relate to grammar. There are no "filler" words.

## Partner Stories
Pairs of students work together to complete a story using specific parts of speech. When they're done, they have a hilariously funny story to share with the class. These activities can be used over and over with new, exciting results each time.

## Crack-the-Code Cloze Games
Students complete a short story by filling in the missing part of speech. Then they use their answers to decode a secret message!

## Riddle Bubble Tests
Students fill in the bubble next to the sentence that uses correct grammar. Then students use their lettered answers to unravel the punch line to an amusing riddle. These riddle tests are not only fun; they're also great practice for state and national standardized tests (students get into the habit of filling in the circle next to the correct answer).

# Enjoy!

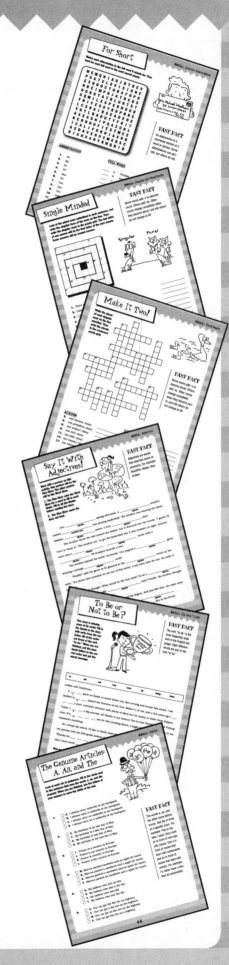

# Noun Hunt

**Read the clues to name the nouns in each list. Then find the nouns in the word search puzzle.**

```
B S H E A C K G T R B A
A C L O U D A F E E M S
P H D G N B I D A S O G
P O F O T N T A C T T M
L O H A C H A F H A H E
E L O B T E B M E U E G
S L M G Q H L W R R R B
T E E N A G E R T A P U
O I A K L K Y R V N C Z
R B I C Y C L E A T I R
E M R B C S I N G E R S
B A I R P O R T M J Z N
```

## PEOPLE

1. An adult who teaches in a classroom  _____
2. Your parents (two words)  _____

    and  _____

3. A person between the ages of 13 and 19  _____
4. A person who sings  _____
5. Your mother's sister is your  _____

## PLACES

6. A place where you buy things  _____
7. A place where you go to learn  _____
8. A place where you go to eat  _____
9. The place where you live  _____
10. A place where planes take off and land  _____

## THINGS

11. A vehicle with two wheels  _____
12. Something you use to carry groceries  _____
13. A fruit that's often red and is used to make pies and juice  _____
14. Something you use at dinner time that comes with chairs  _____
15. Something fluffy that floats in the sky  _____

# Find the Verb

**Read each sentence and underline the verb. Then find each verb in the word search puzzle.**

```
B P H D M A K H A S C I
L A E C A U G H T A O L
M I S B D G I C E L I N
E N S N E S A O F O H V
P T U T Z G V S L V S R
I E B R E O I A H E I E
Y D J W O N U N M S R P
B R O K E M S G S T B C
R F S H A R E D B I H T
L E R V I S I T S D E R
C W A O Q J A O G E Y H
X H R D E A B L E W O E
```

## FAST FACT

Some verbs, like *runs* and *thinks*, describe action. Other verbs, like *is* and *was*, describe a state of being.

1. The play begins at six o'clock.

2. Lucas visits his grandmother at least once a week.

3. The snake caught its prey under a boulder.

4. I read an exciting novel last week.

5. Rebecca painted a picture of a beautiful sunset.

6. My cat is three years old.

7. Our school basketball team just won the state championship.

8. Megan loves pizza with pepperoni.

9. The two brothers shared a seat on the school bus.

10. We sang the national anthem at school today.

11. A rabbit made its nest in our front yard.

12. During the storm, winds blew at speeds of 50 miles per hour.

13. Jared listens to many kinds of music.

14. Anne broke her arm last winter.

15. That film has terrific special effects.

# Verbs Help Out

Read each sentence and locate the helping verb. When you are finished, find your answers in the word search puzzle.

```
A F M I G H T E B P A R E
D O I H B M C L D I O E G
C L Q W E R E R S J S U A
S E O N E T A K H C D I D
H A D T N P V B O S F W T
D U T G Q O M N U U R H E
A B N J W Y W A L I M A S
V A I D C H A R D L Q S E
C M K T F K S N L G C O S
L R S X A M U H D I D N T
P U A O S B V U N P Z B I
M S I H A V E J E R A H I
B W T O E D S V P T Y O F
```

## FAST FACT

Helping verbs help the main verb describe the action. There are 23 helping verbs. They are:

| am | could | have | should |
|----|-------|------|--------|
| are | did | is | was |
| be | do | may | were |
| been | does | might | will |
| being | had | must | would |
| can | has | shall | |

**HELPING VERB**

1. Our neighbors were playing loud music last night. _____

2. You should say thank you to Uncle Roy for the gift. _____

3. I can see the park from my bedroom window. _____

4. My train is leaving in ten minutes. _____

5. I am planning to join the swim team. _____

6. I knew that you owned a dog, but I did not know that you owned a fish. _____

7. Yes, I do like to work with clay. _____

8. I have started my homework. _____

9. My cousins are visiting for the weekend. _____

10. Julia has written a poem for class. _____

11. I was walking to school when I saw an injured bird. _____

12. I might win the contest. _____

13. Tina had just fallen asleep when the telephone rang. _____

# Good, Better, Best

Read each sentence. On the line, write the positive, comparative, or superlative form of the missing adjective. Then find each of your answers in the word search puzzle.

```
A H S D Y B R O C U P E
L M C M N E L O U D E R
H B E O A K C G T N D I
A D A L N R J M E A B S
R T R F A S T E R C P A
D A L O V H E K F O N Z
E A I A E T Y I D L E H
R I E O C L O S E S T B
P S R T A L L E S T E D
U B A Y R C O L D E S T
```

1. Nora was fast, but Caitlyn was _____.
   _(comparative of **fast**)_

2. Snowball is _____ than the other kittens
   _(comparative of **cute**)_
   in the litter.

3. Kevin is _____.
   _(positive of **smart**)_

4. January is the _____ month of the year.
   _(superlative of **cold**)_

5. I filled the _____ glass I could find with water.
   _(superlative of **tall**)_

6. Someone must have turned up the volume, because the

   music suddenly got _____.
   _(comparative of **loud**)_

7. The _____ clouds were a sign that the storm
   _(positive of **dark**)_
   was on its way.

8. Today's math assignment is _____ than
   _(comparative of **hard**)_
   yesterday's.

9. David has an _____ bedtime than I do.
   _(comparative of **early**)_

10. Tina is my _____ friend.
    _(superlative of **close**)_

## FAST FACT

A positive adjective lets you describe one or more things: A puppy is nice; puppies are nice. A comparative adjective lets you compare two or more things: Barbara is nicer than Gerard; Gerard is nicer than all the other boys in our class. A superlative adjective lets you describe only one thing: Mount Everest is the tallest mountain in the world; Remo is the friendliest person in school.

# Noun Substitutes

Read each sentence and fill in each blank with a pronoun from the lists. When you are finished, find your answers in the word search puzzle.

```
A O U R S M C L B H E D A
I B H C N P S A H X I T D
O M R E D T G F M E N H G
E L Y A I K C O W B L E I
J Q H O S I R E Q J G M L
H E D S H E V C A S R K O
K U T E G W T N I T S E R
R X S P R C H B E H L M U
D F M I A F E M K E T S Z
B H E R E Y I D F Y H I M
P H M A L U R A Q S Z R M
T R U J O T B R E C P E T
N U F Y I G C M Y D A H Q
```

## FAST FACT

Pronouns take the place of nouns  Here are some:

| | | | |
|---|---|---|---|
| I | it | him | who |
| you | we | her | what |
| he | me | us | |
| she | they | them | |

Pronouns can be possessive, just like nouns:

| | | |
|---|---|---|
| her/hers | mine | their/theirs |
| his | my | whose |
| its | our/ours | your/yours |

1. " _____ am happy to meet you," I said.

2. Ryan has a doctor's appointment after school, so _____ will miss practice.

3. She baked the cake for so long, _____ was as hard as a rock!

4. Frank and Erin said _____ would be back in one hour.

5. I just saw a man run down the street. Did you see _____?

6. The fourth graders invited _____ to their holiday party, so we will invite them to _____.

7. Mary, do _____ walk to school or ride the bus?

8. Elizabeth hopes _____ will get the lead in the school play.

9. Our family is very busy, but _____ always try to eat dinner together.

10. I reminded Derek that _____ owes me a dollar.

11. When I saw Aunt Sue get off the train, I hugged _____ and offered to carry her bags.

12. The children were misbehaving, so Mrs. Nelson asked _____ to quiet down.

13. I know that's _____ lunch because it has my name on it.

14. A kitten must stay with _____ mother for several weeks.

15. The twins invited all of _____ friends to the birthday party.

# Contraction Action

Read each sentence, paying special attention to the contraction.
On the line, write the word that completes each contraction.
Then find each of your answers in the word search puzzle.

```
A N E A R E H B M I S
H F X I J O E A G D R
K A U N L A C N V U A
D Q D T E S F I T E Q
A H B N O T G E I T U
C I N W Z E R A S L I
O S E F V G U J G I P
L I Y A T V E H A G W
G N H M F S W I L L E
P A E U C O N B D P D
U M C H S K E A I R O
```

## FAST FACT

A contraction is formed
by putting two words
together and leaving out
some letters. An apos-
trophe takes the place
of the missing letters.

1. I couldn't make it to the dance recital on Wednesday.

    couldn't = could + _____

2. Peter should've called if he were going to be late.

    should've = should + _____

3. I'm the oldest child in my family.

    I'm = I + _____

4. Maura was tired because she'd been working in the garden all day.

    she'd = she + _____

5. Edward says he'll be over in ten minutes.

    he'll = he + _____

6. You're my best friend.

    You're = You + _____

7. He's afraid of spiders.

    He's = He + _____

8. 'Twas the night before Christmas.

    'Twas = _____ + was

9. Let's go out to dinner tonight.

    Let's = Let + _____

# For Short

Match each abbreviation to the full word it stands for. Then hunt for each full word in the word search puzzle.

```
W E M Q N I A D J R T R E V
P U A T E L E V I S I O N E
E X N D O C T O R A F O P O
N B E I M P H J A T D C G S
N G K O T A T R L U N T S T
S Q M I L E S P E R H O U R
Y H I F E S D Y B D P B R E
L C S R A I R S E A O E H E
V K T L B A D G T Y F R I T
A S E A U N I P Q A Z U K L
N E R N H O F J E S T M C E
I C A L I F O R N I A E R B
A X D A V E N U E M A B S C
D J A N U A R Y R W Q B I B
```

## FAST FACT

An abbreviation is a shortened version of a word or phrase. Some abbreviations use periods, but others do not.

| | ABBREVIATION | | | FULL WORD |
|---|---|---|---|---|
| 1. | Dr. | ____ | a. | October |
| 2. | Mr. | ____ | b. | Avenue |
| 3. | St. | ____ | c. | Doctor |
| 4. | TV | ____ | d. | Saturday |
| 5. | Jan. | ____ | e. | miles per hour |
| 6. | PA | ____ | f. | television |
| 7. | Ave. | ____ | g. | California |
| 8. | Sat. | ____ | h. | Mister |
| 9. | Oct. | ____ | i. | Street |
| 10. | mph | ____ | j. | United States |
| 11. | U.S. | ____ | k. | Pennsylvania |
| 12. | CA | ____ | l. | January |

# Single Minded

Look at the plural noun underlined in each sentence, and write the singular form of the noun on the line. Then write the singular noun in the puzzle grid. The last letter of one answer will be the first letter of the next answer. Some answers will go around corners.

## FAST FACT

Some nouns add -s to become plural. Others add -es. Other nouns change completely when they become plural, and still others do not change at all!

```
 _____
| 1 |   |   |   |   | 2 |   |
|___|___|___|___|___|___|___|
|   | 8 |   |   | 9 |   |   |
|   |___|___|___|___|___|   |
|   |   |   |   |   |   |   |
|   |   |   |   |   |   |   |
| 7 | 13|   |14 |██ |10 | 3 |
|   |   |   |███|   |   |   |
|   |   |   |   |   |   |   |
|   | 12|   | 11|   |   | 4 |
|   |___|___|___|___|___|   |
| 6 |   |   |   | 5 |   |   |
|___|___|___|___|___|___|___|
```

Singular

Plural

1. There are nine <u>planets</u> in our solar system. _____

2. Cars and <u>trucks</u> lined the street. _____

3. I can't find my house <u>keys</u> anywhere! _____

4. Many homes have back <u>yards</u>. _____

5. There are <u>ditches</u> on both sides of the road. _____

6. It's fun to ride a bike over the <u>hills</u> in this neighborhood. _____

7. Plants have chemicals in their <u>leaves</u> to help them make food. _____

8. Graciela is just under five <u>feet</u> tall. _____

9. Our class has gone on three field <u>trips</u> this school year. _____

10. I save <u>pennies</u> in a jar in my bedroom. _____

11. Does your family eat <u>yams</u> at Thanksgiving? _____

12. Fifty <u>men</u>, women, and children were left homeless by the storm. _____

13. I have a pocket full of <u>nickels</u>. _____

14. Bright <u>lights</u> filled the sky. _____

# In the Past

Rewrite each sentence in the past tense. Then write each past-tense verb in the snail puzzle. The last letter of one answer will be the first letter of the next answer. Some answers will go around corners.

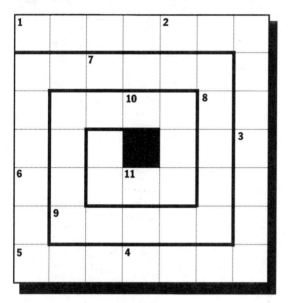

## FAST FACT

The past tense is used to describe something that happened before now. Many verbs form the past tense by adding -ed or -d. But other verbs form the past tense in unusual ways and should be memorized.

**1.** I sleep in a bed.

_____

**2.** She turns the key.

_____

**3.** We decide what to eat for lunch.

_____

**4.** Stephan draws a picture.

_____

**5.** I win the spelling bee!

_____

**6.** Rachel nods her head in agreement.

_____

**7.** They drive to school every day.

_____

**8.** The nurse examines the patient.

_____

**9.** Everyone dances to that song.

_____

**10.** I dare you to watch the scary movie.

_____

**11.** We do the dishes.

_____

# Pick a Preposition

Read each sentence below, and choose a preposition from the box to fill in the blank. Then write the prepositions in the snail puzzle. In the puzzle, the last letter of one answer is the first letter of the next answer. Some answers will go around corners.

## FAST FACT

Prepositions usually tell where something is, where something is going, or when something is happening. Some common prepositions are:

| | | |
|---|---|---|
| about | after | with |
| near | throughout | to |
| below | because | despite |
| without | beside | instead |
| in | over | on |
| except | toward | onto |

**1.** South America is located _____ the Equator.

**2.** You cannot bake a cake _____ flour.

**3.** The sprinter ran _____ the finish line.

**4.** We played outside for a while _____ the cold weather.

**5.** I like all vegetables _____ for lima beans.

**6.** Basketball is popular _____ the entire United States.

**7.** Hannah sent a thank-you note _____ her grandmother.

**8.** Will you help me load the heavy box _____ the truck?

**9.** Anthony lives _____ North Birchfield Avenue.

**10.** The twins live _____ the school, so they do not ride the schoolbus.

# Create-a-Word

Read each clue below and figure out the compound word that is being described. Then write the compound words in the snail puzzle. The last letter of one answer will be the first letter of the next answer. Some answers go around corners.

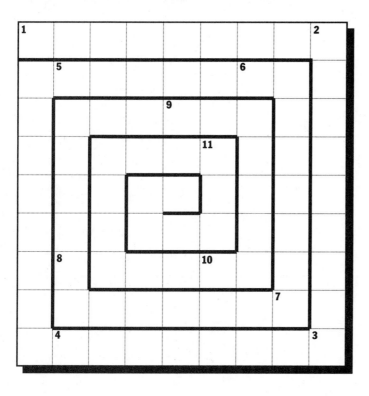

## FAST FACT

A compound word is a word that is made up of two or more smaller words. For example: *notebook, newspaper, thunderstorm.*

## CLUES

**1.** A mark your foot leaves in snow or mud. _____

**2.** These fall from your eyes when you are sad. _____

**3.** At night we have moonlight; in the day we have _____

**4.** A natural disaster that makes the ground shake. _____

**5.** The skin that closes over your eye. _____

**6.** You turn this to open a door. _____

**7.** A sport played with a bat and ball. _____

**8.** All the years that a person lives. _____

**9.** The hard covering around an egg. _____

**10.** A house that warns ships of danger. _____

**11.** A piece of jewelry you wear on your ear. _____

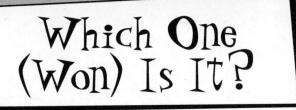

# Which One (Won) Is It?

Read each of the sentences below, and underline the homonym that makes sense in each one. Then write the correct homonyms in the snail puzzle. The last letter of one answer will be the first letter of the next answer. Some answers will go around corners.

Ant    Aunt Betty

## FAST FACT

Homonyms are words that sound alike but have different spellings and meanings. For example: peace/piece and bare/bear.

**1.** My (aunt, ant) is coming to visit for a few weeks.

**2.** Jack likes to play soccer (to, too, two).

**3.** We will eat lunch in about (one, won) hour.

**4.** Rosa's brother is (ate, eight) years old.

**5.** Nigel (threw, through) the ball to first base.

**6.** Room 16 is having a spelling test next (weak, week).

**7.** I don't (know, no) where I left my backpack.

**8.** How much does your puppy (way, weigh)?

**9.** The frightened campers (herd, heard) a noise in the forest.

**10.** The (dear, deer) drank from the cool stream.

**11.** The principal's office is the third door on the (right, write).

**12.** (There, They're, Their) favorite movie is showing tonight at 8 p.m.

**13.** The audience filled 100 (rose, rows) of seats.

**14.** Lori's arm was (sore, soar) after her softball game.

# Do They Agree?

Read each of the sentences below, and underline the verb that agrees with the subject. Then write the correct verbs in the snail puzzle. The last letter of one answer will be the first letter of the next answer. Some answers will go around corners.

|   |   |   |
|---|---|---|
| 1 | 2 | 3 |

(snail puzzle grid with numbers 1, 2, 3, 8, 9, 13, 4, 7, 14, 10, 12, 11, 6, 5)

1. Bears (has, have) a powerful sense of smell.
2. We (eat, eats) out about twice a month.
3. He always (try, tries) to do his homework before dinner.
4. On the island, the sun (shine, shines) almost every day.
5. The recipe (says, say) to cook the muffins for 25 minutes.
6. They (swim, swims) in the lake every afternoon.
7. I (make, makes) the best lemonade in town!
8. Ralph (earn, earns) money by mowing his neighbor's lawn.
9. The kids often (swing, swings) at the playground.
10. My house plants (grows, grow) an inch every month.
11. Henry (were, was) in charge of the class party.
12. At lunch time, Rita always (sit, sits) near the windows.
13. They (switch, switches) seats every week.
14. Christopher (has, have) on a striped sweater today.

## FAST FACT

If the subject of a sentence is singular, the verb must also be singular. If the subject is plural, the verb must be plural. Here's a secret, though: While a noun that ends in -s is usually plural, a verb that ends in -s is usually singular!

# Make It Two!

Write the plural of each singular noun on the line provided. Then write the plurals in the crossword puzzle grid.

## FAST FACT

Some nouns add -s to become plural. Others add -es. Other nouns change completely when they become plural, and still others do not change at all!

## ACROSS

3. one banana; many _____

5. one president; many _____

8. one subject; many _____

9. one itch; many _____

11. one disk; many _____

14. one tomato; many _____

17. one television; many _____

## DOWN

1. one plant; many _____

2. one waitress; many _____

4. one foot; many _____

6. one deer; many _____

7. one note; many _____

10. one child; many _____

12. one cookie; many _____

13. one person; many _____

15. one key; many _____

16. one mouse; many _____

22

# Invisible Nouns

**Use a noun from the box to fill in the blank in each sentence. Then write your answers in the crossword puzzle.**

## FAST FACT

Some nouns name ideas or feelings that you cannot see, hear, smell, or touch. Some examples are happiness, wonder, and justice. These nouns are called abstract nouns.

| | |
|---|---|
| love | respect |
| sadness | anger |
| beauty | fairness |
| democracy | concern |
| sharing | courage |
| hope | courage |
| confidence | intelligence |
| | kindness |

## ACROSS

**4.** Madison has _____ that the future will be bright.

**6.** Jack has _____ in his ability to play soccer.

**8.** The students had great _____ for their teacher.

**9.** For the sake of _____, Marianne gave each child the same number of cookies.

**11.** Caroline's main _____ after the hurricane was the safety of her neighbors.

**12.** Josh treats everyone with _____, so he has many friends.

**13.** When Grandpa saw what the burglars had done to the house, he was filled with _____ .

## DOWN

**1.** Felicia was filled with _____ when her dog died.

**2.** My parents fell in _____ when they were in college.

**3.** The United States government is a _____ .

**5.** In the spring, flowers fill the world with _____ .

**6.** It takes _____ to give a speech in front of the whole class.

**7.** Albert Einstein had _____, but he did not do well in school.

**10.** The kids know that _____ is important. They always take turns with their toys.

# Where's the Action?

Read each sentence and fill in the blank with an action verb from the box. Write the verb in the crossword puzzle.

Balance

**fly**        **wore**
**walked**     **shook**
**won**        **meet**
**opened**     **laughed**
**smiled**     **wrote**
**climbed**    **yelled**
**erased**     **baked**
**led**        **roared**
**carry**      **eat**
**rock**

## FAST FACT

An action verb describes activity that happened in the past, is happening now, or will happen in the future.

## ACROSS

**2.** Jeanette _____ as she thought of the exciting day ahead of her.

**6.** Jack _____ the home-work assignment in his notebook.

**7.** During the earthquake, the whole house _____ .

**9.** Alexis _____ at Courtney's joke.

**10.** Our basketball team _____ the state championship!

**11.** I am so hungry, I could _____ ten pizzas!

**13.** Chris _____ all the way to the top of the tree.

**17.** The lion _____ loudly, surprising the zoo visitors.

**18.** Victor _____ "Fire!" as soon as he saw the flames.

## DOWN

**1.** Samantha _____ her team to victory.

**3.** "I am pleased to _____ you," Jacob said.

**4.** The teacher _____ the writing on the chalk board.

**5.** Don't _____ the boat; it may tip over!

**6.** Gregory _____ the dog around the block.

**8.** I _____ the envelope as soon as I saw it.

**12.** Let's _____ a kite today.

**14.** In honor of your birthday, Aunt Rose _____ a cake.

**15.** My book bag weighs at least 15 pounds. It is too heavy to _____!

**16.** Lucas _____ his favorite tie on school picture day.

# Pronoun Magic

Use a pronoun from the box to fill in the blank in each sentence. You may use some pronouns more than once. Then write the pronouns in the crossword puzzle.

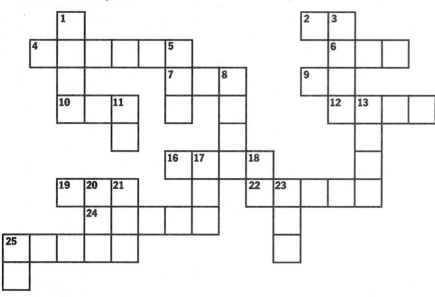

## FAST FACT

Pronouns take the place of nouns:

| | | |
|---|---|---|
| I | it | him |
| you | we | her |
| he | me | us |
| she | they | them |

Pronouns can be possessive, just like nouns:

| | |
|---|---|
| my | their/theirs |
| his | your/yours |
| our/ours | its |
| mine | whose |
| her/hers | |

## ACROSS

**2.** Look at that flower! _____ is beautiful.

**4.** This letter is addressed to my neighbors. It must be _____ .

**6.** Joanna can't wait for the class trip. It will be _____ first visit to a museum.

**7.** George helped me with the science homework. I helped _____ with the math problems.

**9.** Will you join _____ for a walk? I would enjoy your company.

**10.** If you don't hurry, _____ are going to be late for school.

**12.** Can you find _____ way home from here?

**16.** Our school has two playgrounds. Everyone works to keep _____ clean.

**19.** Brian forgot _____ lunch today.

**22.** Is this backpack _____? It has your initials on it.

**24.** The Smiths took _____ new puppy for a walk.

**25.** _____ jacket is this?

## DOWN

**1.** Mike and Rob went to the park because _____ wanted to play ball.

**3.** The students have recess after _____ eat lunch.

**5.** Amanda loves space, so _____ wants to become an astronaut.

**8.** That pen belongs to me. It is _____ .

**11.** A cat followed Bob and me home. It stayed behind _____ the whole way!

**13.** The blue car belongs to our family. The van is _____, too.

**17.** Mrs. Miller remembers every solo _____ daughter sang.

**18.** I was in a rush, so I asked the waiter to bring _____ food quickly.

**20.** Many nutrients of an apple are in _____ peel.

**21.** My mom knows me well. _____ can tell when I've had a bad day.

**23.** My friends and I love to ride bikes. It is _____ favorite activity.

**25.** My brother and I hope _____ both make the soccer team.

# Awesome Adverbs

Read each sentence and fill in the blank with an adverb from the box. Then write your answers in the crossword puzzle.

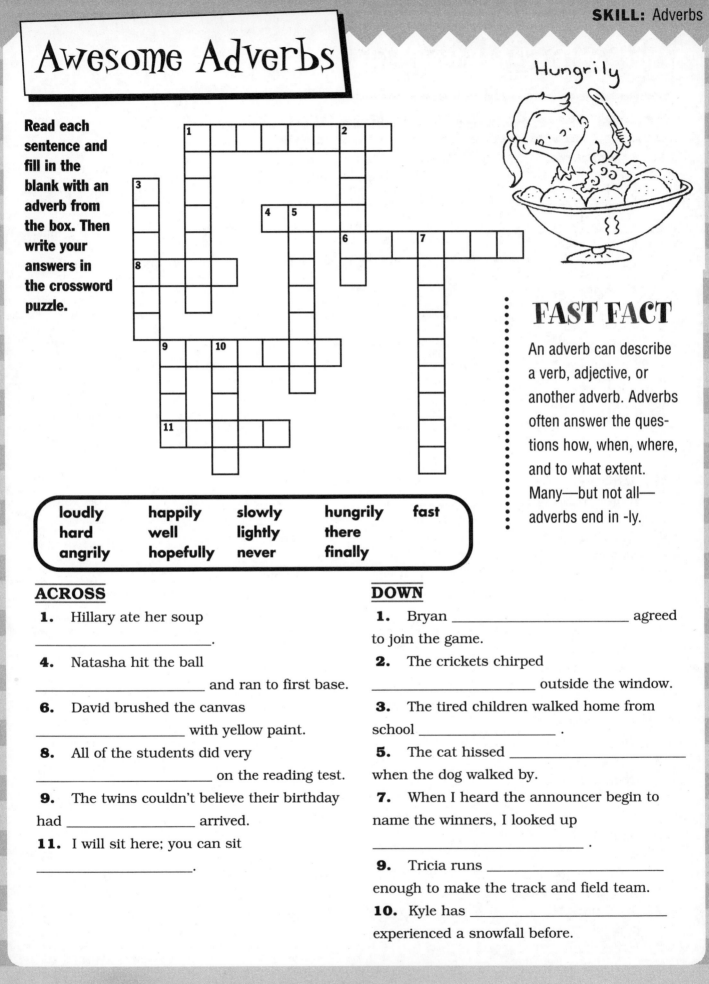

Hungrily

FAST FACT

An adverb can describe a verb, adjective, or another adverb. Adverbs often answer the questions how, when, where, and to what extent. Many—but not all—adverbs end in -ly.

loudly    happily    slowly    hungrily    fast
hard      well       lightly   there       
angrily   hopefully  never     finally

## ACROSS

1. Hillary ate her soup _____.

4. Natasha hit the ball _____ and ran to first base.

6. David brushed the canvas _____ with yellow paint.

8. All of the students did very _____ on the reading test.

9. The twins couldn't believe their birthday had _____ arrived.

11. I will sit here; you can sit _____.

## DOWN

1. Bryan _____ agreed to join the game.

2. The crickets chirped _____ outside the window.

3. The tired children walked home from school _____ .

5. The cat hissed _____ when the dog walked by.

7. When I heard the announcer begin to name the winners, I looked up _____ .

9. Tricia runs _____ enough to make the track and field team.

10. Kyle has _____ experienced a snowfall before.

26

# It's Only Proper

Use a proper adjective from the box to fill in the blank in each sentence. Then write the answers in the puzzle.

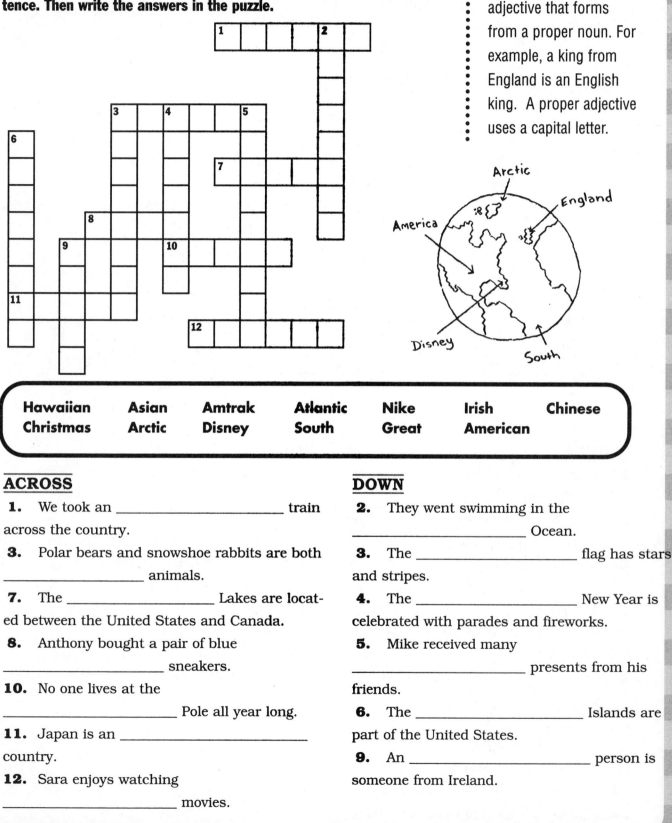

## FAST FACT

A proper adjective is an adjective that forms from a proper noun. For example, a king from England is an English king. A proper adjective uses a capital letter.

| Hawaiian | Asian | Amtrak | Atlantic | Nike | Irish | Chinese |
| Christmas | Arctic | Disney | South | Great | American | |

## ACROSS

**1.** We took an _____ train across the country.

**3.** Polar bears and snowshoe rabbits are both _____ animals.

**7.** The _____ Lakes are located between the United States and Canada.

**8.** Anthony bought a pair of blue _____ sneakers.

**10.** No one lives at the _____ Pole all year long.

**11.** Japan is an _____ country.

**12.** Sara enjoys watching _____ movies.

## DOWN

**2.** They went swimming in the _____ Ocean.

**3.** The _____ flag has stars and stripes.

**4.** The _____ New Year is celebrated with parades and fireworks.

**5.** Mike received many _____ presents from his friends.

**6.** The _____ Islands are part of the United States.

**9.** An _____ person is someone from Ireland.

# Subject Search

**Read each sentence and underline the word that is the simple subject. Write the word in the crossword puzzle.**

## ACROSS

1. They knew that they were going to be late for the meeting.
2. Teachers have exciting jobs.
4. She owns several rare books.
5. The local newspaper ran an article about helping the environment.
7. My new shoes gave me painful blisters.
8. The tall brown mare guarded her new-born foal.
9. The hot sun scorched the farmer's crops.
11. Mrs. Edwards' store closes at 7:30 p.m. on weeknights.
12. It is almost summer time.
13. Cheese is a popular pizza topping.
14. The letter arrived in yesterday's mail.

## DOWN

1. Travis rode the roller coaster four times.
2. The telephone rang loudly.
3. A single star shone in the night sky.
6. Everyone shouted "Surprise!" when Nathan walked in the front door.
8. Beautiful music played while we worked on our projects.
9. Shelly is one of my closest friends.
10. Litter makes the park ugly.

# Food Fight!

**Work with a partner on this activity. One partner will be the Clue Giver. The other partner will be the Word Giver.**

**1. The Clue Giver asks the Word Giver for a word to fill in each blank. Fill in all the blanks before reading the story.**

**2. The Clue Giver reads the story out loud.**

## FAST FACT

Common nouns are general names for people, places, and things. They do not use capital letters. For example: student, home, and apple.

One day the students in our class were having a quiet lunch in the _____.
<br>common noun/place

At first everything was going smoothly. The kids were enjoying fried _____,
<br>common noun/thing

baked _____, and a variety of other tasty treats.
<br>common noun/thing

Trouble started when one of the students was carrying her tray to her seat. Her stomach

grumbled as she gazed at the _____, _____, and
<br>common noun/thing       common noun/thing

_____ on her tray. A _____ and _____
<br>common noun/thing       common noun/person       common noun/person

sitting nearby both looked hungrily at the piping hot lunch. Suddenly, the student tripped on a

_____ on the floor, and her tray went flying. A large _____
<br>common noun/thing       common noun/thing

landed on a _____ who was walking by. "You know what that means!" anoth-
<br>common noun/person

er student shouted. "Food fight!"

Before long, the kids' lunches were sailing through the air. A burned _____
<br>common noun/thing

plopped down on a _____. A greasy _____ flew out
<br>common noun/person       common noun/thing

the window and headed for the _____. The food fight continued until a
<br>common noun/place

mushy _____ sailed right into the teacher.
<br>common noun/thing

"Stop this nonsense," the teacher cried. "Each one of you is behaving like a

_____. Clean up this mess right now or I will send you to the
<br>common noun/person

_____!" Needless to say, that was the end of the food fight!
<br>common noun/place

# The Strangest Field Trip Ever

**Work with a partner on this activity. One partner will be the Clue Giver. The other partner will be the Word Giver.**

**1. The Clue Giver asks the Word Giver for a word to fill in each blank. Fill in all the blanks before reading the story.**

**2. The Clue Giver reads the story out loud.**

## FAST FACT

Proper nouns are the names of specific people, places, and things. They always begin with a capital letter. For example: George, Texas, and the Statue of Liberty.

Last night I had a very unusual dream. In my dream, _____ was the

                                               *proper noun/person*

principal of our school! One day, the principal announced that we were going on a field trip to

_____. Now, I had been to _____ and to _____,
   *proper noun/place*                                  *proper noun/place*                   *proper noun/place*

but never there!

Believe it or not, my dream got even crazier after that. We rode a _____
                                                   *proper noun/form of transportation*

all the way to our destination. Once we arrived, we met all kinds of people. I personally saw

_____ and _____ and even got _____ to give
   *proper noun/person*                *proper noun/person*                   *proper noun/person*

me an autograph. I will always treasure it!

On the way home, we talked the principal into stopping in _____ and
                                              *proper noun/place*

_____. We tried to stop in _____, too, but we ran out of time.
   *proper noun/place*                          *proper noun/place*

Even so, it was the most awesome field trip I had ever been on. Was I ever disappointed when it

was time to wake up!

# Alien Adventure

**Work with a partner on this activity. One partner will be the Clue Giver. The other partner will be the Word Giver.**

**1. The Clue Giver asks the Word Giver for a word to fill in each blank. Fill in all the blanks before reading the story.**

**2. The Clue Giver reads the story out loud.**

## FAST FACT

The present tense describes an action that is happening now. The past tense describes an action that already happened. Many verbs form the past tense by adding -ed or -d.

When I saw the flashing lights, I knew right away it was a

UFO. It_____ right next to me. The doors opened, and out came _____
    verb/past tense                                         number over 2

_____. The creatures marched toward me and began to speak. "We are from the
plural noun

planet _____," they said. "We travel around the Milky Way, stopping only to
    noun

_____. Tell us about yourself, Earthling."
verb/present tense

I _____ and I _____. I did not know what to say, "My name
    verb/past tense        verb/past tense

is _____," I began. "I like to _____ and
    word giver's name              verb/present tense

_____. My favorite thing to do is _____ and hang out
    verb/present tense            verb/present tense

with my good friend, _____."
    noun/person's name

The creatures looked at each other and _____. "Aha," they said.
    verb/past tense

"Earth is very different from our planet. Come, and we will show you."

I hopped aboard the UFO and we took off. The creatures and I _____ and
    verb/past tense

_____. They also gave me a delicious _____ to eat.
verb/past tense                   noun/thing

Finally, we arrived. I could tell we were there when the UFO _____. I
                                verb/past tense

stepped outside. I watched as alien creatures _____ and _____.
           verb/past tense       verb/past tense

I was homesick already, without my family and my favorite _____. "Take me
          noun

home!" I told the aliens. They shrugged and put me back on the UFO—by myself! "Wait" I cried.

"I don't know how to fly this thing!"

The doors closed, and I spied a control panel. I did not know which button to press, so I

just _____. Amazingly, the UFO _____ and started its journey back
    verb/past tense       verb/past tense

to Earth. It took me _____ days, but I finally made it home.
    number

# I See the Future

**Work with a partner on this activity. One partner will be the Clue Giver.
The other partner will be the Word Giver.**

**1. The Clue Giver asks the Word Giver for a word to fill in each blank. Fill
in all the blanks before reading the story.**

**2. The Clue Giver reads the story out loud.**

**FAST FACT**

To form the future
tense, verbs add the
word will. For example:
He will run tomorrow.

What will life on Earth be like 100 years from now? Here's what I think:

People _____ much less often than they do today, but they
_____ verb/future tense

_____ at least ten times a day. Children _____ in
verb/future tense                                                    verb/future tense

schools and they _____ in their neighborhoods.
verb/future tense

   In the United States, most people _____ , but in other parts of the
verb/future tense

world, people _____ . People everywhere _____ .
verb/future tense                                        verb/future tense

   In the future, all cars _____ and bikes _____ . It
verb/future tense                          verb/future tense

will be so much fun! Computers _____ , and machines _____ .
verb/future tense                                  verb/future tense

   What will I be doing 100 years from now? Thanks to medical advances, I will still be

around. I probably _____ , and I definitely _____ . But most
verb/future tense                                verb/future tense

of all I _____ ! I can hardly wait!
verb/future tense

# Say It With Adjectives!

**Work with a partner on this activity. One partner will be the Clue Giver. The other partner will be the Word Giver.**

**1. The Clue Giver asks the Word Giver for a word to fill in each blank. Fill in all the blanks before reading the story.**

**2. The Clue Giver reads the story out loud.**

## FAST FACT

Adjectives are words that describe nouns or pronouns. For example: beautiful, sloppy, blue, broken.

One _____ spring afternoon, a _____ student
          *adjective*                             *adjective*

named _____ was playing basketball. The student was wearing the latest
     *noun/first name*

fashion: _____ pants and a very _____ shirt.
       *adjective*                          *adjective*

The student threw the ball toward the basket, but it bounced into the woods. "I guess I'll

have to chase it." The student ran to get the basketball but it was nowhere in sight. Instead,

there was a _____ , _____ bottle with a
        *adjective*               *adjective*

_____ lid propped beneath a tree.
    *adjective*

The student opened the bottle cautiously. Out popped a _____ genie
                                             *adjective*

wearing a strange _____ outfit!
                 *adjective*

"Finally!" said the genie as he glanced at the _____ watch on his
                                          *adjective*

wrist. "It's about time someone let me out of this bottle. I only have time for one wish. So make

it snappy."

The student thought. What would be the best wish? To be a _____
                                             *adjective*

superstar? To have some really _____ toys? Finally, the student thought
                         *adjective*

of the perfect wish and told the genie.

"Whatever," said the genie as he snapped his fingers. And just like that, the wish came

true. The student became a _____ , _____
                         *adjective*                         *adjective*

_____ , and never forgot that _____ day in the forest.
   *noun*                                        *adjective*

# A Parts-of-Speech Circus

**Work with a partner on this activity. One partner will be the Clue Giver. The other partner will be the Word Giver.**

**1. The Clue Giver asks the Word Giver for a word to fill in each blank. Fill in all the blanks before reading the story.**

**2. The Clue Giver reads the story out loud.**

## FAST FACT

A noun is a person, place or thing (Mr. Simpson, Ohio, banana ). A verb tells the action in the sentence (lifts, dances, sees). An adjective describes a noun (blue, nice, smart). An adverb usually describes a verb (quickly, happily, wildly).

Last week, the circus came to our town. It was set up near the

old _____. I wasn't planning to go, but
     *common noun/place*

_____ and _____ talked me into it. They were dying to see the
  *proper noun/person*               *proper noun/person*

_____ _____ and the _____
   *adjective*           *common noun/thing*             *adjective*

_____ .
  *common noun/person*

When we arrived, we were starving, so we got in line to buy some snacks.

I ate the _____ _____, and my friends ate the
      *adjective*         *common noun/thing*

_____ _____.
  *adjective*       *common noun/thing*

Then the show began. The ringmaster _____ announced the first act.
                              *adverb*

Then _____ _____ came out and started to _____
   *adjective/number*     *plural noun*                  *verb/present tense*

_____! When the act was over, everyone began to _____
  *adverb*                                *verb/present tense*

_____ and _____ _____ .
  *adverb*       *verb/present tense*       *adverb*

Later in the show, we saw a _____ _____ and a
                       *adjective*       *common noun/thing*

_____ _____ who could _____ and
  *adjective*      *common noun/person*        *verb/present tense*

_____. The best part of the show was the last act, when a _____
 *verb/present tense*                                *adjective*

_____ _____ _____ on top of a _____!
 *common noun/person*    *verb/past tense*    *adverb*            *any common noun*

We ran into _____ and _____. They were carrying a
         *common noun/person*       *common noun/person*

_____ that they had bought as a souvenir. They said they loved the show, too!
 *common noun/thing*

34

# A Pet Adventure

This adventure story is missing its adverbs! Fill in the blanks in the story with adverbs from the box below. When you are finished, put the numbered letters in the correct order and get the secret message.

## FAST FACT

Adverbs can describe verbs, adjectives, or even other adverbs. They usually answer the questions how, when, or where. They often end in the letters -ly.

| suddenly | loudly | high | sadly | fearlessly | wildly |
|----------|--------|------|-------|------------|--------|
| quickly | breathlessly | desperately | hungrily | innocently | |

My neighbors asked me to watch their dog, Sophie. I ___ ___ ___ ___ ___ ___ ___ ___ ___ ___ ___
                                                          1
needed the money, so I took the job. Sophie barked ___ ___ ___ ___ ___ ___ and gave me a
                                                        2
big kiss. I took her by the leash and waved good-bye.

Trouble began when she chewed off her leash and ran ___ ___ ___ ___ ___ ___

down the street. When I caught her, she was licking someone's ice cream cone! Then she

___ ___ ___ ___ ___ ___ ___ ___ ___ ___ ___ ran across the street. I followed
 3        4
___ ___ ___ ___ ___ ___ ___ ___ ___ ___ ___ ___ ___ behind her.
 5

Sophie stopped at the park. There, she ___ ___ ___ ___ ___ ___ ___ made some new
                                             8            6
friends, leaped ___ ___ ___ ___ into the air to grab their Frisbee, and greeted a man who was
                     7
feeding the squirrels.

We were invited to a picnic and ate ___ ___ ___ ___ ___ ___ ___ ___. Then I
                                               9
___ ___ ___ ___ ___ ___ ___ ___ realized it was time to go. We ___ ___ ___ ___ ___ said
10                       11                                            12
good-bye, and got home minutes before Sophie's owners. They saw her sitting

___ ___ ___ ___ ___ ___ ___ ___ ___ ___ by the door and exclaimed. "Sophie's so good for
                         13
you. Are you available next week?"

**Now use the circled letters to decode the message:**

___ ___  ___ ___ ___ ___  ___ ___  ___ ___ ___ ___ ___
 5   1    6   7   9   12   13   2    3   8   4   4   11

___ ___ ___ ___ ___ ___ ___!
 3   4   7   1   9   12   10

# Prepositions Show Position

This story is missing its prepositions! Fill in the blanks in the story with prepositions from the box below. When you are finished, put the numbered letters in the correct order and get the secret message.

| about | before | except | in | near | with | to |
|-------|--------|--------|-----|------|------|-----|
| above | by | from | inside | on | without | |

Last summer, I went ___ ___ Space Camp! I went for three days, ___ ___ ___ ___ a
                        1                                    2   3   4
Monday to a Wednesday. On the first day, I got to try on a space suit just like the ones worn by

real astronauts. It had an American flag ___ ___ the front and all kinds of special equipment

built into it. It even had a device to control the temperature inside the suit.

___ ___ ___ ___ ___ ___ ___ this equipment, astronauts could not survive ___ ___ space.
                    5

The next day, I got to taste astronaut food. I especially liked the freeze-dried ice cream. In

fact, all of the kids at Space Camp (___ ___ ___ ___ ___ ___ for one or two) thought the
                                      6       7
ice cream was the best.

Finally, I got to go ___ ___ ___ ___ ___ ___ a special anti-gravity chamber. It was
                         8       9
invented ___ ___ scientists to give astronauts an idea of what it's like to be weightless in
            10
outer space. While I was floating inside the chamber, I imagined that I was traveling far

___ ___ ___ ___ ___ the Earth. Wow!
11

Before I knew it, it was time to head home. But before I left, I got to meet a real-life astro-

naut. She sat down ___ ___ ___ ___ all the campers and told us ___ ___ ___ ___ ___
                        12                                        13
her job. She sat ___ ___ ___ ___ me, so I even got an autograph! Now I don't just *think* I
                    14
want to be an astronaut. I know for sure!

**Now use the numbered letters to decode the message:**

___ ___ ___ ___ ___   ___ ___ ___   ___ ___ ___ ___
 3   6   11   7   12    2   1   3    10   1   5   3

___ ___ ___ ___ ___ ___!
 9   3   6   13   4   8

36

# A Conjunction's Function

This story is missing its conjunctions! Fill in the blanks in the story with conjunctions from the box below. When you are finished, put the numbered letters in the correct order and get the secret message.

## FAST FACT

Conjunctions are linking words. They join words, phrases, clauses, and sentences together.

| and | or | yet | if | since | before |
|-----|-----|-----|-------|---------|--------|
| but | nor | so | until | because | once |

The day we moved into our new house, the weather was rainy ___ ___ ___ cold.
                                                          1   2

___ ___ ___ ___ ___ I could not play outside, I decided to explore the attic. It was mostly
3

empty, ___ ___ ___ a few dusty boxes sat in the corner, belonging to the previous owners
       4

___ ___ ___ ___ ___ ___ ___ my family had not come up here yet.
              5

I began to look through one of the boxes filled with papers that looked old and fragile, ___ ___

I was careful. I uncovered an old map and recognized our neighborhood. It showed a large "X"

near the lake, at the end of our road. "Hmmmm," I thought to myself. "X" marks the spot." For a

chest full of gold ___ ___ a priceless piece of jewelry? I could hardly wait to find out!
                  6

Luckily the next day was sunny. ___ ___ ___ ___ I finished breakfast, I set out to search
                               7

for the spot marked on my map. ___ ___ ___ ___ ___ ___ I had gotten very far, I heard a
                               8

voice say, "I'm Kate. You must be the new kid." I said "hello." I didn't want Kate to think I was

silly, ___ ___ ___ I knew she might be a big help so I showed her my map. Soon both of us
       9

were having a great time.

We found plenty of garbage, and may never know ___ ___ there is treasure by the lake, but
                                                10

I have a new pal!

**Now use the circled letters to decode the message:**

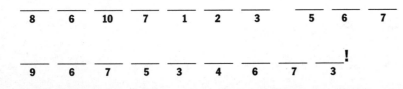

___ ___ ___ ___ ___ ___ ___  ___ ___ ___
 8   6   10   7   1   2   3    5   6   7

___ ___ ___ ___ ___ ___ ___ ___ ___!
 9   6   7   5   3   4   6   7   3

**37**

# Hey, Wow!

This letter is missing its inter-jections! Fill in the blanks in the story with interjections from the box below. When you are finished, put the numbered letters in the correct order and get the secret message.

## FAST FACT

An interjection is a word or phrase that express-es strong feelings. It is usually punctuated with an exclamation point.

| All right | Hello | Thanks | Wow | Hey | Yuck | Oops | Phew |
|-----------|-------|--------|-----|-----|------|------|------|

Dear Aunt Linda,

___ ___ ___ ___ ___ there!  I just got the train set you sent for my birthday.

___ ___ ___ ___ ___ ___!  I really love it. It has eight cars and a long, curving track.
    1    2       3

___ ___ ___!  It has to be the nicest train set I've ever seen.

    It took me about three hours to put the set together (with mom's help). ___ ___ ___ ___!

It sure was hard work! But when I was finally finished, I was very excited. I invited my best

friend, Tim, over to take a look. Tim loves trains as much as I do. When he saw it, he shouted,

"___ ___ ___ ___ ___ ___ ___ ___!"  Tim and I played with the trains for a while. Then
           4           5

Tim's brother, Lou, came over, and we had to put the set away. That's because Lou tried to play

with the track and almost broke it. I said, "___ ___ ___!  Please be careful with that!"
                                     6

    I hear my mom calling me for dinner, so I will wrap up this letter. We are having liver and

lima beans. ___ ___ ___ ___!  I hope you are having something tastier!
           7    8

    I will talk to you soon!

                                Love,

                                Daniel

P.S.: ___ ___ ___ ___!  I almost forgot to tell you that my first soccer game of the season will
     9

be this Saturday morning!

**Now use the numbered letters to decode the message:**

___ ___ ___ ___ ___ ___ ___ ___ ___ ___ ___!
 3   5   1   6    9   2    5   4   1   7   8

# To Be or Not to Be?

**This story is missing some of its verbs! Fill in the blanks in the story with verbs from the box below. All of the verbs are forms of the verb "to be." When you are finished, put the numbered letters in the correct order and get the secret message.**

| is | am | are | was | were | be | being | been |
|----|----|----|----|----|----|----|----|

Ladies and Gentlemen,

It ___ ___ quite an honor to stand before you this evening and accept this award. I am
<br>   **1**

thrilled to ___ ___ named the Inventor of the Year. Believe it or not, just a few years ago I
<br>      **2**

___ ___ ___ a poor, unknown inventor with plenty of ideas but no money to make them happen.

Today, I ___ ___ a big success, all thanks to my famous Two-In-One Dental Floss and Fishing
<br>       **3**

Line. If it ___ ___ ___ ___ not for this amazing device, I might still be dreaming away in my
<br>    **4**

basement workshop.

As I accept my award, I'd like to thank some special people in my life. They ___ ___ ___
<br>                                                            **5**   **6**

my parents and my fifth-grade science teacher, Mrs. C. A. Labrat. To all three of them, I say,

"Thanks for ___ ___ ___ ___ there for me!" And to all of you in the audience, I say
<br>                    **7**

that I have never ___ ___ ___ ___ happier or more proud than I am tonight.
<br>                **8**

**Now use the numbered letters to decode the message:**

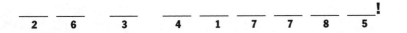

___ ___  ___  ___  ___  ___  ___  ___  ___!
<br>**2**   **6**    **3**    **4**    **1**    **7**    **7**    **8**    **5**

# A Capital Idea

Look at each set of sentences. Fill in the circle next to the sentence that uses capital letters properly. When you are finished, use the letters of your answers to solve the riddle at the end.

1. ○ **A.** The Statue of Liberty is in new york, New York.
   ○ **B.** The Statue of Liberty is in New York, New York.
   ○ **C.** The statue of liberty is in new york, new york.
   ○ **D.** the Statue of Liberty is in New York, New York.

2. ○ **E.** George Washington was america's first president.
   ○ **F.** George Washington was America's first president.
   ○ **G.** George Washington Was America's First President.
   ○ **H.** George washington was america's first president.

3. ○ **I.** Many creatures live in the Pacific Ocean.
   ○ **J.** Many creatures live in the pacific ocean.
   ○ **K.** Many creatures live in the Pacific ocean.
   ○ **L.** Many Creatures live in the Pacific Ocean.

4. ○ **M.** My cat's Name is Lady.
   ○ **N.** My cat's name is Lady.
   ○ **O.** My Cat's name is Lady.
   ○ **P.** My cat's name is lady.

5. ○ **Q.** Where are you celebrating thanksgiving this year?
   ○ **R.** where are you celebrating Thanksgiving this year?
   ○ **S.** Where are you celebrating Thanksgiving this year?
   ○ **T.** Where are you celebrating Thanksgiving this Year?

6. ○ **U.** he and I both go to school with karen.
   ○ **V.** He and I both go to School with Karen.
   ○ **W.** He and I both go to school with Karen.
   ○ **X.** He and i both go to school with Karen.

## FAST FACT

Capital or upper case letters are used to begin proper nouns, to begin sentences, for the personal pronoun I, and in many abbreviations.

**7.**
  ○ **Y.** Mr. bloomberg teaches fourth grade.
  ○ **Z.** Mr. Bloomberg Teaches fourth grade.
  ○ **A.** Mr. Bloomberg teaches fourth grade.
  ○ **B.** MR. Bloomberg teaches Fourth Grade.

**8.**
  ○ **C.** We made a birthday cake for uncle phil.
  ○ **D.** We made a Birthday cake for Uncle Phil.
  ○ **E.** We made a birthday cake for Uncle Phil.
  ○ **F.** We made a birthday Cake for Uncle Phil.

**9.**
  ○ **G.** The Mississippi river sometimes floods.
  ○ **H.** The Mississippi River Sometimes floods.
  ○ **I.** The Mississippi River sometimes floods.
  ○ **J.** the Mississippi River sometimes floods.

**10.**
  ○ **K.** Jennifer has a Girl Scout meeting after school on Monday.
  ○ **L.** Jennifer has a girl scout meeting after school on monday.
  ○ **M.** jennifer has a Girl Scout meeting after school on Monday.
  ○ **N.** Jennifer has a girl Scout meeting after School on Monday.

**11.**
  ○ **O.** They are having a family reunion in March.
  ○ **P.** They are having a Family Reunion in march.
  ○ **Q.** they are having a family reunion in March.
  ○ **R.** They Are having a family reunion in March.

**12.**
  ○ **S.** Playland is Roger's favorite amusement park.
  ○ **T.** Playland is roger's favorite amusement park.
  ○ **U.** playland is Roger's favorite amusement park.
  ○ **V.** Playland is Roger's favorite Amusement park.

**Now solve the riddle! Each number below stands for one of the questions. Write the letter of the correct answer above each number. You will spell out the answer to this riddle:**

Where does a polar bear keep its money?

___ ___  ___  ___  ___  ___  ___  ___  ___  ___  ___!
3   4    7    12   4    11   6    1    7    4    10

# Whose Is It?

Look at each set of sentences. Fill in the circle next to the sentence that uses possessive nouns properly. When you are finished, use the letters of your answers to solve the riddle at the end.

1. ○ **A.** The cats's fur was matted from the rain.
   ○ **B.** The c'ats fur was matted from the rain.
   ○ **C.** The cats fur was matted from the rain.
   ○ **D.** The cat's fur was matted from the rain.

2. ○ **E.** The churchs door is made of thick wood.
   ○ **F.** The churches door is made of thick wood.
   ○ **G.** The church's door is made of thick wood.
   ○ **H.** The churches's door is made of thick wood.

3. ○ **I.** We're going over to Juan's house.
   ○ **J.** We're going over to Juans house.
   ○ **K.** We're going over to Juan house.
   ○ **L.** We're going over to Juans's house.

4. ○ **M.** The childrens toys were all over the floor.
   ○ **N.** The children's toys were all over the floor.
   ○ **O.** The childrens's toys were all over the floor.
   ○ **P.** The children toys' were all over the floor.

5. ○ **Q.** Our classes field trip will be next Thursday.
   ○ **R.** Our class's field trip will be next Thursday.
   ○ **S.** Our classs field trip will be next Thursday.
   ○ **T.** Our class' field trip will be next Thursday.

6. ○ **U.** The Smiths's driveway is very long.
   ○ **V.** The Smiths' driveway is very long.
   ○ **W.** The Smithses driveway is very long.
   ○ **X.** The Smiths driveway is very long.

7. ○ **Y.** The doll's dress is as beautiful as Margarets own outfit.
   ○ **Z.** The dolls' dress is as beautiful as Margaret's own outfit.
   ○ **A.** The doll's dress is as beautiful as Margaret's own outfit.
   ○ **B.** The dolls dress is as beautiful as Margaret's own outfit.

## FAST FACT

A possessive noun shows ownership. Most singular nouns become possessive by adding -'s. Most plural nouns ending in -s become possessive by adding an apostrophe after the -s.

**8.**
- ○ **C.** Bailey's phone number is easy to remember.
- ○ **D.** Baile'ys phone number is easy to remember.
- ○ **E.** Baileys phone number is easy to remember.
- ○ **F.** Baileys's phone number is easy to remember.

**9.**
- ○ **G.** Our store's motto is, "The customers needs come first."
- ○ **H.** Our store's motto is, "The customers's needs come first."
- ○ **I.** Our store's motto is, "The customers' needs come first."
- ○ **J.** Our stores motto is, "The customers' needs come first."

**10.**
- ○ **K.** My brothers jacket is too big for me.
- ○ **L.** My brother' jacket is too big for me.
- ○ **M.** My brothers's jacket is too big for me.
- ○ **N.** My brother's jacket is too big for me.

**11.**
- ○ **O.** I'd like to have a pen like Michelle's.
- ○ **P.** I'd like to have a pen like Michelles.
- ○ **Q.** I'd like to have a pen like Michelles'.
- ○ **R.** I'd like to have a pen like Michelles's.

**12.**
- ○ **S.** Johns and Erics reports were both excellent.
- ○ **T.** John's and Eric's reports were both excellent.
- ○ **U.** John's' and Eric's' reports were both excellent.
- ○ **V.** Johns' and Eric's reports were both excellent.

**13.**
- ○ **W.** Nora's goal improved her teams' chances of winning.
- ○ **X.** Noras goal improved her team's chances of winning.
- ○ **Y.** Nora's goal improved her team's chances of winning.
- ○ **Z.** Noras goal improved her teams chances of winning.

**Now solve the riddle!** Each number below stands for one of the questions. Write the letter of the correct answer above each number. You will spell out the answer to this riddle:

Where does afternoon come before morning?

| 9 | 10 | 7 | 1 | 3 | 8 | 12 | 3 | 11 | 10 | 7 | 5 | 13 |
|---|----|---|---|---|---|----|---|----|----|---|---|----|

# The Genuine Articles: A, An, and The

Look at each set of sentences. Fill in the circle next to the sentence that uses the words *a, an,* and *the* properly. When you are finished, use the letters of your answers to solve the riddle at the end.

1.  ○ **A.** I always carry umbrella in my backpack.
    ○ **B.** I always carry a umbrella in my backpack.
    ○ **C.** I always carry an umbrella in my backpack.
    ○ **D.** I always carry an a umbrella in my backpack.

2.  ○ **E.** My birthday is an last day of May.
    ○ **F.** My birthday is a last day of May.
    ○ **G.** My birthday is last day of May.
    ○ **H.** My birthday is the last day of May.

3.  ○ **I.** France is a country in Europe.
    ○ **J.** France is an country in Europe.
    ○ **K.** France is country in Europe.
    ○ **L.** France is the country in Europe.

4.  ○ **M.** Marcus packed sandwich and an apple for lunch.
    ○ **N.** Marcus packed a sandwich and a apple for lunch.
    ○ **O.** Marcus packed a sandwich and an apple for lunch.
    ○ **P.** Marcus packed an sandwich and a apple for lunch.

5.  ○ **Q.** My balloon rose into an sky.
    ○ **R.** My balloon rose into a the sky.
    ○ **S.** My balloon rose into sky.
    ○ **T.** My balloon rose into the sky.

6.  ○ **U.** Our car got the flat tire on highway.
    ○ **V.** Our car got a flat tire on the highway.
    ○ **W.** Our car got an flat tire on the highway.
    ○ **X.** Our car got flat tire on a highway.

## FAST FACT

The words *a, an,* and *the* often come before nouns. Use *the* in front of a specific noun. For example: This is *the* bike I want. Use *a* and *an* in front of non-specific nouns. Use *a* in front of nouns that start with consonants and *an* in front of nouns that start with vowels. For example: I'd rather have *a* bike than *an* automobile.

**7.** ○ **Y.** Toby's coat has an hood and a zipper.
○ **Z.** Toby's coat has a hood and an zipper.
○ **A.** Toby's coat has a hood and a zipper.
○ **B.** Toby's coat has hood and a zipper.

**8.** ○ **C.** I always try to sit in an front of the bus.
○ **D.** I always try to sit in the front of an bus.
○ **E.** I always try to sit in the front of the bus.
○ **F.** I always try to sit in a front of the bus.

**9.** ○ **G.** A sun is supposed to come out later.
○ **H.** The sun is supposed to come out later.
○ **I.** An sun is supposed to come out later.
○ **J.** A the sun is supposed to come out later.

**10.** ○ **K.** I must read a story and study for a exam.
○ **L.** I must read story and study for an exam.
○ **M.** I must read a story and study for an exam.
○ **N.** I must read an story and study for an exam.

**11.** ○ **O.** They say an apple a day keeps the doctor away.
○ **P.** They say a apple a day keeps the doctor away.
○ **Q.** They say an apple a day keeps an doctor away.
○ **R.** They say a apple an day keeps the doctor away.

**12.** ○ **S.** The Smiths went hiking in the Rocky Mountains.
○ **T.** The Smiths went hiking in a Rocky Mountains.
○ **U.** A Smiths went hiking in the Rocky Mountains.
○ **V.** The Smiths went hiking in an Rocky Mountains.

**Now solve the riddle! Each number below stands for one of the questions. Write the letter of the correct answer above each number. You will spell out the answer to this riddle:**

Where does a cow go in its free time?

___ ___   ___ ___ ___   ___ ___ ___ — ___ ___ ___ ___!
5  4   5  2  8   10  4  11  6  3  8  12

# Using Contractions

Look at each set of sentences. Fill in the circle next to the sentence that uses contractions properly. When you are finished, use the letters of your answers to solve the riddle at the end.

did + not = _____
he + would = _____
can + not = _____

1. ○ **A.** W'ell see you tomorrow.
   ○ **B.** Well see you tomorrow.
   ○ **C.** We'll see you tomorrow.
   ○ **D.** Wel'l see you tomorrow.

2. ○ **E.** Id like to see a movie this weekend.
   ○ **F.** Iw'd like to see a movie this weekend.
   ○ **G.** 'Id like to see a movie this weekend.
   ○ **H.** I'd like to see a movie this weekend.

3. ○ **I.** Ling knew she needed glasses when she cou'ldnt see the board.
   ○ **J.** Ling knew she needed glasses when she couldnt see the board.
   ○ **K.** Ling knew she needed glasses when she could'nt see the board.
   ○ **L.** Ling knew she needed glasses when she couldn't see the board.

4. ○ **M.** Dad said hed pick me up after school.
   ○ **N.** Dad said he'd pick me up after school.
   ○ **O.** Dad said h'ed pick me up after school.
   ○ **P.** Dad said hed' pick me up after school.

5. ○ **Q.** Joseph cant have a dog because he's allergic to fur.
   ○ **R.** Joseph can't have a dog because hes allergic to fur.
   ○ **S.** Joseph ca'nt have a dog because h'es allergic to fur.
   ○ **T.** Joseph can't have a dog because he's allergic to fur.

6. ○ **U.** Sandy is my sister, but she's also my best friend.
   ○ **V.** Sandy is my sister, but sh'es also my best friend.
   ○ **W.** Sandy is my sister, but shes also my best friend.
   ○ **X.** Sandy is my sister, but sh's also my best friend.

## FAST FACT

A contraction is formed by putting two words together and leaving out some letters. An apostrophe takes the place of the missing letters.

**7.**
- ○ **Y.** Ill play basketball after dinner.
- ○ **Z.** Il'l play basketball after dinner.
- ○ **A.** I'll play basketball after dinner.
- ○ **B.** 'Ill play basketball after dinner.

**8.**
- ○ **C.** We tried to move the boulder, but it wouldnt budge.
- ○ **D.** We tried to move the boulder, but it would'nt budge.
- ○ **E.** We tried to move the boulder, but it wouldn't budge.
- ○ **F.** We tried to move the boulder, but it wou'ldnt budge.

**9.**
- ○ **G.** My grandparents said theyd visit, but they didn't say when.
- ○ **H.** My grandparents said the'yd visit, but they didn't say when.
- ○ **I.** My grandparents said they'd visit, but they didn't say when.
- ○ **J.** My grandparents said th'eyd visit, but they didn't say when.

**10.**
- ○ **K.** Ive always wanted to travel around the world.
- ○ **L.** Ive' always wanted to travel around the world.
- ○ **M.** I've always wanted to travel around the world.
- ○ **N.** Iv'e always wanted to travel around the world.

**11.**
- ○ **O.** Don't forget to bring a jacket!
- ○ **P.** Dont forget to bring a jacket!
- ○ **Q.** D'ont forget to bring a jacket!
- ○ **R.** Do'nt forget to bring a jacket!

**12.**
- ○ **S.** Lets ask the librarian for help finding the book.
- ○ **T.** Lets' ask the librarian for help finding the book.
- ○ **U.** Let's ask the librarian for help finding the book.
- ○ **V.** Le'ts ask the librarian for help finding the book.

**Now solve the riddle! Each number below stands for one of the questions. Write the letter of the correct answer above each number. You will spell out the answer to this riddle:**

When is an astronaut's favorite time to eat?

___ ___ ___ ___ ___ ___    ___ ___ ___ ___!
 3   7   6   4   1   2      5   9   10   8

# Be Agreeable!

Look at each set of sentences. Fill in the circle next to the sentence in which the subject and verb agree. When you are finished, use the letters of your answers to solve the riddle at the end.

1.
- ○ **A.** Janine plays in the school band.
- ○ **B.** Janine play in the school band.
- ○ **C.** Janine were playing in the school band.
- ○ **D.** Janine are playing in the school band.

2.
- ○ **E.** I lives about six blocks from Sam's apartment building.
- ○ **F.** I live about six blocks from Sam's apartment building.
- ○ **G.** I are living about six blocks from Sam's apartment building.
- ○ **H.** I is living about six blocks from Sam's apartment building.

3.
- ○ **I.** That book is one of my sister's favorites.
- ○ **J.** That book are one of my sister's favorites.
- ○ **K.** That book am one of my sister's favorites.
- ○ **L.** That book were one of my sister's favorites.

4.
- ○ **M.** Mirtha's favorite topics is birds and plants.
- ○ **N.** Mirtha's favorite topics was birds and plants.
- ○ **O.** Mirtha's favorite topics are birds and plants.
- ○ **P.** Mirtha's favorite topics am birds and plants.

5.
- ○ **Q.** Dogs love water, but cats hates it.
- ○ **R.** Dogs love water, but cats hate it.
- ○ **S.** Dogs loves water, but cats hates it.
- ○ **T.** Dogs loves water, but cats hate it.

6.
- ○ **U.** A tornado strike our area once every few years.
- ○ **V.** A tornado strikes our area once every few years.
- ○ **W.** Tornadoes strikes our area once every few years.
- ○ **X.** Tornadoes is striking our area once every few years.

## FAST FACT

If the subject of a sentence is singular, the verb must also be singular. If the subject is plural, the verb must be plural.

**7.**
- ◯ **Y.** Owen am bringing chips and salsa to the party.
- ◯ **Z.** Owen are bringing chips and salsa to the party.
- ◯ **A.** Owen is bringing chips and salsa to the party.
- ◯ **B.** Owen bringing chips and salsa to the party.

**8.**
- ◯ **C.** The Philadelphia Eagles has a talented coach.
- ◯ **D.** The Philadelphia Eagle have a talented coach.
- ◯ **E.** The Philadelphia Eagles have a talented coach.
- ◯ **F.** The Philadelphia Eagles has had a talented coach.

**9.**
- ◯ **G.** Benjamin and Matthew goes to the same swim club.
- ◯ **H.** Benjamin and Matthew is going to the same swim club.
- ◯ **I.** Benjamin and Matthew go to the same swim club.
- ◯ **J.** Benjamin and Matthew am going to the same swim club.

**10.**
- ◯ **K.** Traffic on the highway have been backed up for five miles.
- ◯ **L.** Traffic on the highway is backed up for five miles.
- ◯ **M.** Traffic on the highway are backed up for five miles.
- ◯ **N.** Traffic on the highway am backed up for five miles.

**11.**
- ◯ **O.** My aunt knows a lot about current events because she am a reporter.
- ◯ **P.** My aunt knows a lot about current events because she are a reporter.
- ◯ **Q.** My aunt know a lot about current events because she is a reporter.
- ◯ **R.** My aunt knows a lot about current events because she is a reporter.

**12.**
- ◯ **S.** The cafeteria often run out of ice cream, and the students get disappointed.
- ◯ **T.** The cafeteria often runs out of ice cream, and the students gets disappointed.
- ◯ **U.** The cafeteria often run out of ice cream, and the students gets disappointed.
- ◯ **V.** The cafeteria often runs out of ice cream, and the students get disappointed.

**Now solve the riddle! Each number below stands for one of the questions. Write the letter of the correct answer above each number. You will spell out the answer to this riddle:**

What has a mouth but cannot smile?

___  ___ ___ ___ ___ ___!
 7    11   3   6   8   5

# Is It a Sentence?

Look at each set of answers. Fill in the circle next to the answer that is a complete sentence. When you are finished, use the letters of your answers to solve the riddle at the end.

1. 
   ○ **A.** Chicken for dinner.
   ○ **B.** We are having chicken for dinner.
   ○ **C.** Having chicken for dinner.
   ○ **D.** We chicken for dinner.

2. 
   ○ **E.** Did the mail arrive yet?
   ○ **F.** The mail?
   ○ **G.** Mail yet?
   ○ **H.** Did arrive yet?

3. 
   ○ **I.** The park opens at seven o'clock in the morning.
   ○ **J.** At seven o'clock in the morning.
   ○ **K.** The park at seven o'clock in the morning.
   ○ **L.** At seven o'clock in the morning, the park.

4. 
   ○ **M.** Enough apples to make an apple pie.
   ○ **N.** We picked enough apples to make an apple pie.
   ○ **O.** Picked enough apples to make an apple pie.
   ○ **P.** We apples to make an apple pie.

5. 
   ○ **Q.** A new CD.
   ○ **R.** Got a new CD for her birthday.
   ○ **S.** Lori a new CD for her birthday.
   ○ **T.** Lori got a new CD for her birthday.

6. 
   ○ **U.** Please close the door behind you.
   ○ **V.** The door behind you.
   ○ **W.** The door behind you, please.
   ○ **X.** Behind you.

## FAST FACT

A sentence must have a subject and a verb. In a command, the subject is understood to be "you." For example: (You) Answer the phone, please!

**7.**
- ○ **Y.** Since the weather is so nice.
- ○ **Z.** The window.
- ○ **A.** Let's open the window, since the weather is so nice.
- ○ **B.** The window, since the weather is so nice.

**8.**
- ○ **C.** How to play softball at summer camp.
- ○ **D.** Kelly learned how to play softball at summer camp.
- ○ **E.** Kelly how to play softball at summer camp.
- ○ **F.** To play softball.

**9.**
- ○ **G.** Which movie would you like to see?
- ○ **H.** Which movie?
- ○ **I.** Like to see?
- ○ **J.** Which movie would like to see?

**10.**
- ○ **K.** Mr. Finley a math teacher for fourteen years.
- ○ **L.** A math teacher for fourteen years.
- ○ **M.** For fourteen years, Mr. Finley.
- ○ **N.** Mr. Finley has been a math teacher for fourteen years.

**11.**
- ○ **O.** Filled the sky just before noon.
- ○ **P.** Just before noon, dark clouds.
- ○ **Q.** Just before noon.
- ○ **R.** Just before noon, dark clouds filled the sky.

**12.**
- ○ **S.** Natalie, who already knows French.
- ○ **T.** Natalie, who already knows French, plans to study Spanish next year.
- ○ **U.** Natalie to study Spanish next year.
- ○ **V.** To study Spanish next year.

**Now solve the riddle! Each number below stands for one of the questions. Write the letter of the correct answer above each number. You will spell out the answer to this riddle:**

What do grizzlies do when they are having a bad day?

<u>    </u> <u>    </u> <u>    </u> <u>    </u>    <u>    </u> <u>    </u> <u>    </u>    <u>    </u> <u>    </u> <u>    </u> <u>    </u>    <u>    </u> <u>    </u>!
 9    11    3    4       7    10    8       1    2    7    11       3    12

# Be a Comma Cop!

Look at each set of sentences. Fill in the circle next to the sentence that uses commas properly. When you are finished, use the letters of your answers to solve the riddle at the end.

1.   ○ **A.** I'd like a hamburger, salad, and milk for supper.
     ○ **B.** I'd like a hamburger salad and milk for supper.
     ○ **C.** I'd like a hamburger salad and, milk for supper.
     ○ **D.** I'd like, a hamburger, salad, and milk for supper.

2.   ○ **E.** Louisa has a pair of red white and blue shorts.
     ○ **F.** Louisa has a pair, of red, white and blue shorts.
     ○ **G.** Louisa has a pair of red, white, and blue shorts.
     ○ **H.** Louisa has a pair of red white, and blue, shorts.

3.   ○ **I.** The shopkeeper said "Everything is on sale,"
     ○ **J.** The, shopkeeper said, "Everything is on sale."
     ○ **K.** The shopkeeper said "Everything, is, on sale."
     ○ **L.** The shopkeeper said, "Everything is on sale."

4.   ○ **M.** I was born on May 23 1991.
     ○ **N.** I was, born on May 23, 1991.
     ○ **O.** I was born on May, 23, 1991.
     ○ **P.** I was born on May 23, 1991.

5.   ○ **Q.** My favorite cousins live in, Los Angeles California.
     ○ **R.** My favorite cousins, live, in Los Angeles, California.
     ○ **S.** My favorite cousins live in Los Angeles California.
     ○ **T.** My favorite cousins live in Los Angeles, California.

6.   ○ **U.** The cake smelled delicious, which made the children hungry.
     ○ **V.** The cake smelled delicious which made the children hungry.
     ○ **W.** The cake smelled delicious which made the children, hungry.
     ○ **X.** The cake smelled delicious which, made the children hungry.

## FAST FACT

Commas are used to separate items in a list, to separate a quotation from the rest of the sentence, to separate a city from a state or country, to separate the month and day from the year, and to separate clauses in a sentence.

**7.**   ◯ **Y.** Grown-ups, kids, and animals all enjoyed the good weather.
   ◯ **Z.** Grown-ups, kids, and animals, all enjoyed the good weather.
   ◯ **A.** Grown-ups kids and animals all enjoyed the good weather.
   ◯ **B.** Grown-ups kids, and animals all enjoyed the good weather.

**8.**   ◯ **C.** The next century will begin on January 1 2100.
   ◯ **D.** The next century will begin on January 1, 2100.
   ◯ **E.** The next century will, begin on January 1 2100.
   ◯ **F.** The next century will begin on January, 1, 2100.

**9.**   ◯ **G.** My chores are to make my bed clean my room and set the table for dinner.
   ◯ **H.** My chores are to make my bed, clean my room and set the table for dinner.
   ◯ **I.** My chores are to make my bed, clean my room, and set the table for dinner.
   ◯ **J.** My chores are to, make my bed clean my room and, set the table for dinner.

**10.**   ◯ **K.** Mr. Linnett, the principal of our school, is very funny.
   ◯ **L.** Mr. Linnett the principal of our school is very funny.
   ◯ **M.** Mr. Linnett the principal of, our school, is very funny.
   ◯ **N.** Mr. Linnett, the principal of our school is, very funny.

**11.**   ◯ **O.** Brett wanted to be here, today but he, has the flu.
   ◯ **P.** Brett wanted to be here today, but he has the flu.
   ◯ **Q.** Brett wanted to be here today, but, he, has the flu.
   ◯ **R.** Brett wanted, to be here today but he has the flu.

**12.**   ◯ **S.** Grandma grew up in Bismarck, North Dakota.
   ◯ **T.** Grandma grew up in Bismarck North Dakota.
   ◯ **U.** Grandma grew up in Bismarck North, Dakota.
   ◯ **V.** Grandma grew up in, Bismarck North Dakota.

**Now solve the riddle! Each number below stands for one of the questions. Write the letter of the correct answer above each number. You will spell out the answer to this riddle:**

What flowers have big mouths?

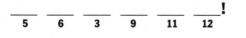

‾‾ ‾‾ ‾‾ ‾‾ ‾‾ ‾‾!
5   6   3   9   11  12

# Sentence Enders

Look at each set of sentences. Fill in the circle next to the sentence that is punctuated properly. When you are finished, use the letters of your answers to solve the riddle at the end.

1.
   ○ **A.** We stayed at the park for one hour,
   ○ **B.** We stayed at the park for one hour.
   ○ **C.** We stayed at the park for one hour?
   ○ **D.** We stayed at the park for one hour

2.
   ○ **E.** Help! There's a fire!
   ○ **F.** Help. There's a fire.
   ○ **G.** Help. There's a fire?
   ○ **H.** Help! There's a fire

3.
   ○ **I.** Do you know the capital of California.
   ○ **J.** Do you know the capital of California!
   ○ **K.** Do you know the capital of California?
   ○ **L.** Do you know the capital of California

4.
   ○ **M.** Is Francine home sick today.
   ○ **N.** Is Francine home sick today!
   ○ **O.** Is Francine home sick today
   ○ **P.** Is Francine home sick today?

5.
   ○ **Q.** My name is Colin?
   ○ **R.** My name is Colin.
   ○ **S.** My name is. Colin
   ○ **T.** My name is Colin!?

6.
   ○ **U.** Marigolds need a lot? of sun.
   ○ **V.** Marigolds need a lot of sun
   ○ **W.** Marigolds need a lot of sun.
   ○ **X.** Marigolds need a lot of sun,

## FAST FACT

A statement ends in a period. (.) A question ends in a question mark. (?) A strong command or an exclamation ends in an exclamation point. (!)

**7.**
- ○ **Y.** Stop, thief?
- ○ **Z.** Stop, thief
- ○ **A.** Stop, thief!
- ○ **B.** Stop, thief.

**8.**
- ○ **C.** Wearing sunscreen protects your skin from dangerous rays
- ○ **D.** Wearing sunscreen protects your. skin from dangerous rays
- ○ **E.** Wearing sunscreen protects your skin from dangerous rays.
- ○ **F.** Wearing sunscreen protects your skin from dangerous rays?

**9.**
- ○ **G.** What time will the next train depart?
- ○ **H.** What time will the next train depart
- ○ **I.** What time will the next train depart!
- ○ **J.** What time will the next train depart.

**10.**
- ○ **K.** Zachary rides a green mountain bike
- ○ **L.** Zachary rides a green mountain bike.
- ○ **M.** Zachary rides a green mountain bike,?
- ○ **N.** Zachary rides a green mountain bike:

**11.**
- ○ **O.** I just won a million dollars
- ○ **P.** I just won a million dollars,
- ○ **Q.** I just won a million dollars.?
- ○ **R.** I just won a million dollars!

**12.**
- ○ **S.** Would you like to share a snack
- ○ **T.** Would you like to share a snack?
- ○ **U.** Would you like to share a snack!
- ○ **V.** Would you like to share a snack.

**Now solve the riddle! Each number below stands for one of the questions. Write the letter of the correct answer above each number. You will spell out the answer to this riddle:**

Who gets paid for loafing around?

___   ___ ___ ___ ___ ___!
7      1     7    3    8   11

# Quotation Location

"Hello!"

"How are you?"

Look at each set of sentences. Fill in the circle next to the sentence that uses quotation marks properly. When you are finished, use the letters of your answers to solve the riddle at the end.

1.
- A. "Please open the letter, said Jeffrey."
- B. "Please open the letter, said Jeffrey.
- C. "Please open the letter," said Jeffrey.
- D. Please open the letter, said Jeffrey."

2.
- E. Our national anthem is The Star-Spangled Banner.
- F. Our national anthem is "The Star-Spangled Banner.
- G. Our national anthem is The Star-Spangled Banner."
- H. Our national anthem is "The Star-Spangled Banner."

3.
- I. "I was on TV!" Lucy exclaimed.
- J. "I was on TV! Lucy exclaimed."
- K. I was on TV! Lucy exclaimed.
- L. "I was on TV! Lucy exclaimed.

4.
- M. The umpire shouted, "You're out!
- N. The umpire shouted, "You're out!"
- O. The umpire shouted, You're out!
- P. "The umpire shouted, You're out!"

5.
- Q. Chapter 4 is called A New Beginning.
- R. "Chapter 4" is called A New Beginning.
- S. Chapter 4 is called A New Beginning."
- T. Chapter 4 is called "A New Beginning."

6.
- U. "Will you join me for lunch? Gil asked.
- V. Will you join me for lunch? Gil asked.
- W. "Will you join me for lunch?" Gil asked.
- X. "Will you join me for lunch? Gil asked."

**FAST FACT**

Quotation marks go around a person's exact words. They also set apart the titles of songs and poems and the titles of chapters in books. Quotation marks always come in pairs.

**7.**
- ○ **Y.** "Check the card catalog, the librarian suggested.
- ○ **Z.** Check the card catalog the librarian suggested.
- ○ **A.** "Check the card catalog," the librarian suggested.
- ○ **B.** "Check the card catalog, the librarian suggested."

**8.**
- ○ **C.** Jody's favorite saying is, Live and let live."
- ○ **D.** Jody's favorite saying is, Live and let live.
- ○ **E.** Jody's favorite saying is, "Live and let live."
- ○ **F.** "Jody's favorite saying is, Live and let live."

**9.**
- ○ **G.** The poem is called, "The Hilltop."
- ○ **H.** The poem is called The Hilltop.
- ○ **I.** The poem is called, The Hilltop.
- ○ **J.** The poem is called, The Hilltop."

**10 .**
- ○ **K.** The clerk asked may I help you find something?
- ○ **L.** The clerk asked, May I help you find something?
- ○ **M.** The clerk asked, "May I help you find something?"
- ○ **N.** The clerk asked, "May I help you find something?

**11.**
- ○ **O.** I pledge allegiance to the flag, the class recited.
- ○ **P.** "I pledge allegiance to the flag," the class recited.
- ○ **Q.** "I pledge allegiance to the flag, the class recited.
- ○ **R.** "I pledge allegiance to the flag, the class recited."

**12.**
- ○ **S.** Donald asked, "What time is it?" and Lora answered, Ten thirty.
- ○ **T.** Donald asked, What time is it? and Lora answered, Ten thirty.
- ○ **U.** Donald asked, "What time is it? and Lora answered, Ten thirty."
- ○ **V.** Donald asked, "What time is it?" and Lora answered, "Ten thirty."

**Now solve the riddle! Each number below stands for one of the questions. Write the letter of the correct answer above each number. You will spell out the answer to this riddle:**

What animal always wins at a game of cards?

___    ___ ___ ___ ___ ___ ___ ___!
 7      1   2   8   8   5   7   2

# Answer Key

## WORD SEARCH PUZZLES

### Noun Hunt (page 9)

### Verbs Help Out (page 11)

### Find the Verb (page 10)

### Good, Better, Best (page 12)

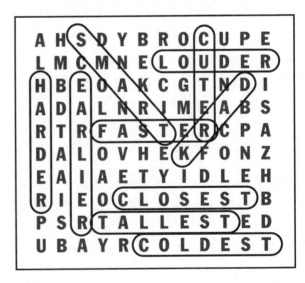

## Noun Substitutes (page 13)

## For Short (page 15)

## SNAIL ("WRAPAROUND") PUZZLES

## Contraction Action (page 14)

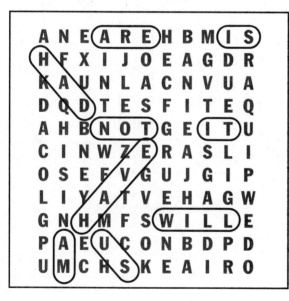

## Single Minded (page 16)

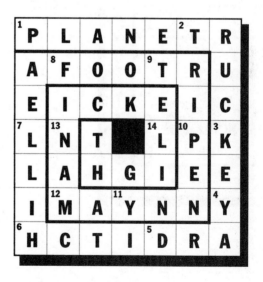

**In the Past** (page 17)

```
S L E P T U R
D E D R O V N
D C E D A E E
O N D █ R X D
N A I D E A E
O D E N I M C
W E R D E D I
```

**Create a Word** (page 19)

```
F O O T P R I N T T
K E Y E L I D O E
A T I M E G G O A
U E O U S E S R R
Q F H N G A H K D
H I T I R R E N R
T L H G I L L O
R L A B E S A B P
A E N I H S N U S
```

**Pick a Preposition** (page 18)

```
B E L O W I T
C E P T H R H
X O N E A O O
E T █ R U U
T N █ G T
I O T U O H O
P S E D R A W
```

**Which One (Won) Is It?** (page 20)

```
A U N T O O N
I G H E A R E
E I R O W D I
W E █ S E G
O H E R O E H
N T H G I R T
K E E W E R H
```

## Do They Agree? (page 21)

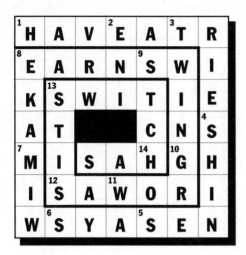

## Invisible Nouns (page 23)

## CROSSWORD PUZZLES

### Make It Two! (page 22)

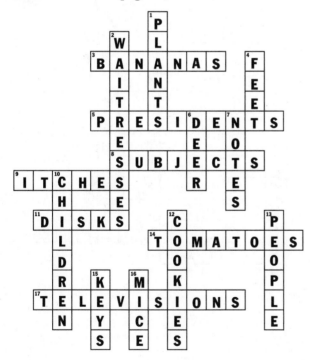

### Where's the Action? (page 24)

## Pronoun Magic (page 25)

## It's Only Proper (page 27)

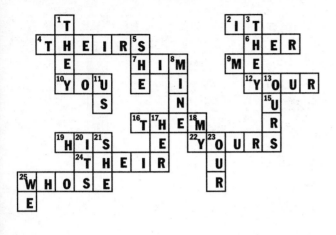

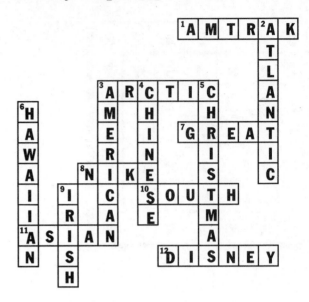

## Awesome Adverbs (page 26)

## Subject Search (page 28)

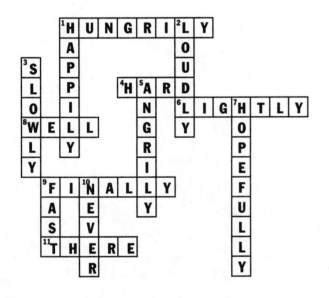

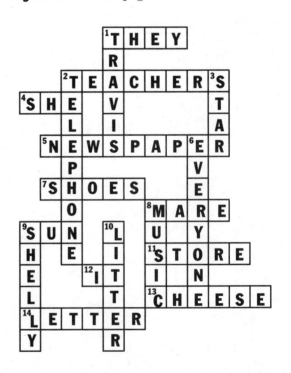

## PARTNER STORIES

### Food Fight!
(page 29): Answers will vary.

### The Strangest Field Trip Ever
(page 30): Answers will vary.

### Alien Adventure
(page 31): Answers will vary.

### I See the Future!
(page 32): Answers will vary.

### Say It With Adjectives
(page 33): Answers will vary.

### A Parts-of-Speech Circus
(page 34): Answers will vary.

## CRACK-THE-CODE STORIES

Answers are listed in the order they appear in the stories.

### A Pet Adventure (page 35): desperately, loudly, wildly, fearlessly, breathlessly, quickly, high, hungrily, suddenly, sadly, innocently.
**Message: Be kind to furry friends.**

### Prepositions Show Position (page 36): to, from, on, without, in, except, inside, by, above, with, about, near. **Message: Reach for your dreams.**

### A Conjunction's Function
(page 37): and, since, but, because, so, or, once, before, yet, if. **Message: Friends are treasures.**

### Hew, Wow! (page 38): hello, thanks, wow, phew, all right, hey, yuck, oops. **Message: Stay on track.**

### To Be or Not To Be (page 39): is, be, was, am, were, are, being, been. **Message: Be a winner.**

## RIDDLE BUBBLE TESTS

### A Capital Idea (page 40): 1. B; 2. F; 3. I; 4. N; 5. S; 6. W; 7. A; 8. E; 9. I; 10. K; 11. O; 12. S.
**Riddle: In a snowbank.**

### Whose Is It? (page 42): 1. D; 2. G; 3. I; 4. N; 5. R; 6. V; 7. A; 8. C; 9. I; 10. N; 11. O; 12. T; 13. Y.
**Riddle: In a dictionary.**

### The Genuine Articles (page 44): 1. C; 2. H; 3. I; 4. O; 5. T; 6. V; 7. A; 8. E; 9. H; 10. M; 11. O; 12. S. **Riddle: To the moo-vies.**

### Using Contractions (page 46): 1. C; 2. H; 3. L; 4. N; 5. T; 6. U; 7. A; 8. E; 9. I; 10. M; 11. O; 12. U.
**Riddle: launch time.**

### Be Agreeable (page 48): 1. A; 2. F; 3. I; 4. O; 5. R; 6. V; 7. A; 8. E; 9. I; 10. L; 11. R; 12. V.
**Riddle: A river.**

### Is It a Sentence? (page 50): 1. B; 2. E; 3. I; 4. N; 5. T; 6. U; 7. A; 8. D; 9. G; 10. N; 11. R; 12. T.
**Riddle: Grin and bear it.**

### Be a Comma Cop! (page 52): 1. A; 2. G; 3. L; 4. P; 5. T; 6. U; 7. Y; 8. D; 9. I; 10. K; 11. P; 12. S.
**Riddle: tulips.**

### Sentence Enders (page 54): 1. B; 2. E; 3. K; 4. P; 5. R; 6. W; 7. A; 8. E; 9. G; 10. L; 11. R; 12. T.
**Riddle: A baker.**

### Quotation Location (page 56): 1. C; 2. H; 3. I; 4. N; 5. T; 6. W; 7. A; 8. E; 9. G; 10. M; 11. P; 12. V.
**Riddle: A cheetah.**

# Notes